UNSOLVED

# LOCH NESS MONSTER

DINAH WILLIAMS

Children's Press®

An imprint of Scholastic Inc.

A special thank-you to our team of fact-checkers.



Library of Congress Cataloging-in-Publication Data available

ISBN 978-1-5461-7860-6 (library binding) | ISBN 978-1-5461-7861-3 (paperback)

10 9 8 7 6 5 4 3 2 1 26 27 28 29 30

Printed in China 62

First edition, 2026

Book design by Kay Petronio

Photos ©: cover: John R. Foster/Science Source; back cover background: Bettmann/Getty Images; back cover top: Dale O'Dell/Alamy Images; 1: John R. Foster/Science Source; 2–3 background: Bettmann/Getty Images; 2 bottom left: Victor Habbick Visions/Science Source; 4: John R. Foster/Science Source; 5: Jim McMahon/Mapman ®; 6–7: Daniel Eskridge/Getty Images; 9: Tony Hobbs/Alamy Images; 10: Fortean/TopFoto; 11: Dale O'Dell/Alamy Images; 12: Mirrorpix/Getty Images; 13: Gregory Sweeney/Getty Images; 14: Ullstein bild/Getty Images; 15: Rko/Kobal/Shutterstock; 16, 17: Daily Mail/Shutterstock; 18–19: Historia/Shutterstock; 20: Buffalo Courier Express/Newspapers.com; 21: Clipart Library; 22: The Granger Collection; 23: Rue des Archives/The Granger Collection; 24: John Redman/AP Images; 25: Rolls Press/Popperfoto/Getty Images; 28: Axel Heimken/picture alliance/Getty Images; 32: Legend of Loch Ness/YouTube; 33: Peter Jolly/Shutterstock; 34: Richard Outdoors/YouTube; 36: VILN visitinvernesslochness/Eoin O Faodhagain; 37: UNPIXS; 40: VICTOR HABBICK VISIONS/Science Source; 41 top: Fortean/TopFoto; 41 center left, center right, bottom left: Peter Jolly/Northpix; 41 bottom right: The Loch Ness Centre / SWNS; 42–43: VICTOR HABBICK VISIONS/Science Source; 44 top left: Fortean/TopFoto; 44 top center: Ullstein bild/Getty Images; 44 top right: Historia/Shutterstock; 44 bottom left: Mirrorpix/Getty Images; 44 bottom right: Daily Mail/Shutterstock; 45 top left: The Granger Collection; 45 top right: UNPIXS; 45 bottom left: Rolls Press/Popperfoto/Getty Images; 45 bottom right: Peter Jolly/Shutterstock; 46 top: Hoberman Collection/Universal Images Group/Getty Images; 46 bottom: Dave Pape/Wikimedia.

All other photos © Shutterstock.

CONTENTS

INTRODUCTION

# MONSTER MYSTERY

Loch Ness is a large, deep lake in Scotland. The water is home to a lot of marine life. But some people believe there is something unusual living in the lake.

Many people claim they have seen a monster in Loch Ness. It is a mysterious creature. It is said to have a long neck and a huge body. There are photos and videos of the creature. But are they real?

## WHERE IS LOCH NESS?

*Loch* is the Scottish word for "lake." The name *Ness* is taken from the River Ness. The river connects the lake to the North Sea.

If the Loch Ness monster is real, what is it? The creature could be a type of **prehistoric** marine reptile. The plesiosaur lived in the water around Scotland. It was thought to be around 40 feet (12 m) long.

The plesiosaur had a long neck and sharp teeth.

But the plesiosaur went **extinct** 66 million years ago. The monster could also be a type of fish. Many people think the creature is a giant eel. But there is no evidence or proof of that.

The Loch Ness monster is a famous attraction. Tourists visit Scotland from all over the world. They want to spot the creature known as "Nessie." Visitors can ride on popular boat cruises around Loch Ness.

Loch Ness is more than 22 miles (35 km) long. A boat cruise around the lake takes about an hour.

About one million tourists visit Loch Ness each year.

Local restaurants and shops make money from tourists. Some might want to keep the stories alive for the visitors. Is the Loch Ness monster real or a **hoax**? Let's explore what we know!

CHAPTER 1

# THE FIRST SIGHTINGS

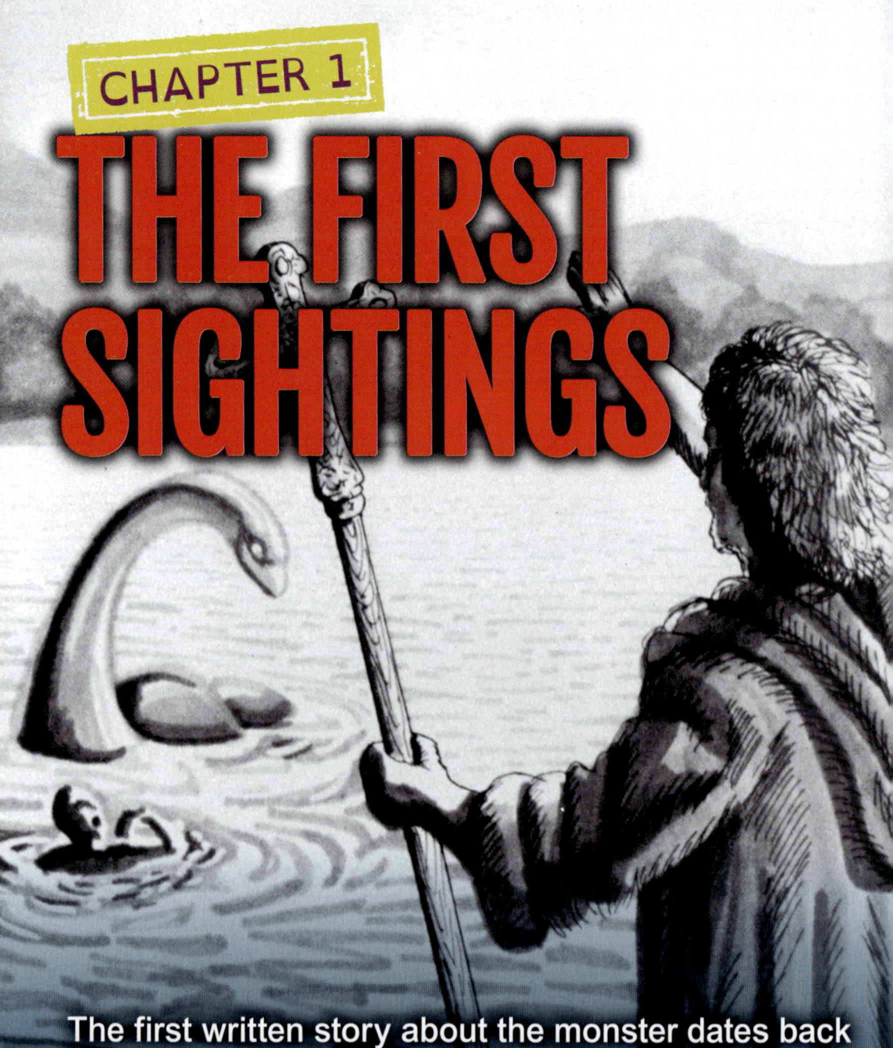

The first written story about the monster dates back to 565 **CE**. It took place in the River Ness. A man had just been killed by a water beast. A **monk** was passing by. His name was Saint Columba.

Saint Columba confronting the water beast.

The story says Saint Columba brought the man back to life. Then he saw the beast rise out of the water. Columba made the sign of the cross. He yelled, "You will go no further!" He drove the beast into the lake. The local people thought it was a miracle.

The creature wasn't called the "Loch Ness monster" until 1933.

Since Columba, only a few sightings had been reported. Until the Loch Ness monster made news in May 1933. Aldie Mackay and her husband were driving near Loch Ness. They stopped when they saw a huge creature. It was swimming in the lake.

Mackay told a local newspaper. She claimed its body was as big as a whale. It made massive waves when it dove into the water!

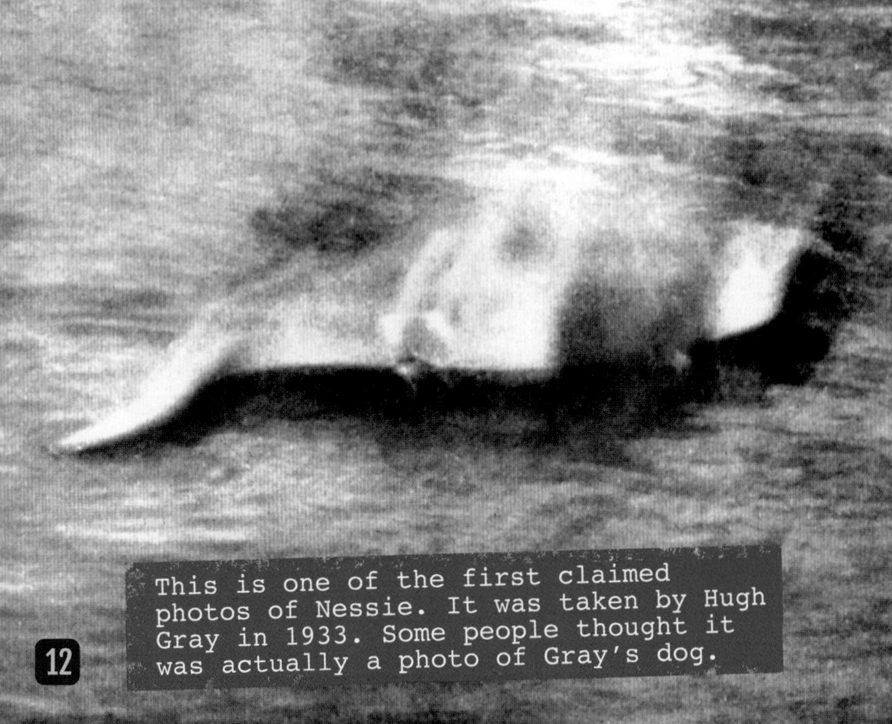

This is one of the first claimed photos of Nessie. It was taken by Hugh Gray in 1933. Some people thought it was actually a photo of Gray's dog.

# MERMAID OR MAMMALS?

Many tales from history had mysterious creatures that were not real. Sometimes, animals were mistaken for other creatures. For example, sailors told stories about mermaids. Their stories were told for thousands of years. The mermaids were later revealed to be manatees. Manatees are large sea mammals.

Manatees can be found in warm coastal waters and rivers.

The monster was spotted again three months later. George Spicer and his wife were driving back from vacation. Suddenly, they came across a large creature. It was crossing the road.

Spicer described the creature in a letter. He sent the letter to a local newspaper. "It seemed to have a long neck," he wrote. "And the body was fairly big, with a high back." It moved quickly across the road. Then it disappeared into the lake.

This is another photo said to be of the Loch Ness monster from 1933. The building on the right is called Urquhart Castle.

## HOAX ALERT!

The creature Spicer described was like one from a movie. A brontosaurus appeared in *King Kong*. The movie came out in 1933 and was very popular. Some people believe the Spicers made up their story. They got the idea from the movie.

This is the brontosaurus from *King Kong*. Spicer didn't have a photograph of the creature he described. Do you think he was telling the truth?

Duke Wetherell

Duke Wetherell was a well-known hunter. A British newspaper hired him to find the Loch Ness monster. Wetherell traveled to the lake and quickly found tracks. In his report, he said they were from an animal nearly 20 feet (6 m) long.

Wetherell made **casts** of the tracks. They were sent to London's Natural History Museum. The museum said they were *not* from a monster. They were from a giant stuffed hippopotamus foot. It was believed that Wetherell made the foot and tracks himself.

Wetherell (right) also searched the lake for Nessie. Here he is loading supplies onto a boat.

Robert Kenneth Wilson made the most famous claim. He was a surgeon from England. Wilson said he was driving near Loch Ness in April 1934. He noticed something in the water. The head of a strange animal was rising out of the waves.

This is Wilson's photo. It became the most well-known image of the Loch Ness monster.

Wilson quickly took four photos. One captured the beast. He sent the photo to a newspaper. It showed the monster's head and long neck sticking out of the water. Many people thought this photo was proof that the monster was real!

The popular image became known as the "Surgeon's Photo." People believed the photo was real for almost sixty years!

Loch Ness Monster Photographed

Reports of the Surgeon's Photo were in many Scottish newspapers.

# HOAX ALERT!

Years later, the truth came out! It was revealed that Wetherell, the hunter, faked the Surgeon's Photo. He and his family had built a phony monster. They took photos of it. Then they convinced Wilson to claim he took the photo himself. Wilson submitted it to the newspaper. In 1991, Wetherell's family admitted to the hoax. Wilson's photo was fake. But it didn't mean there wasn't a monster.

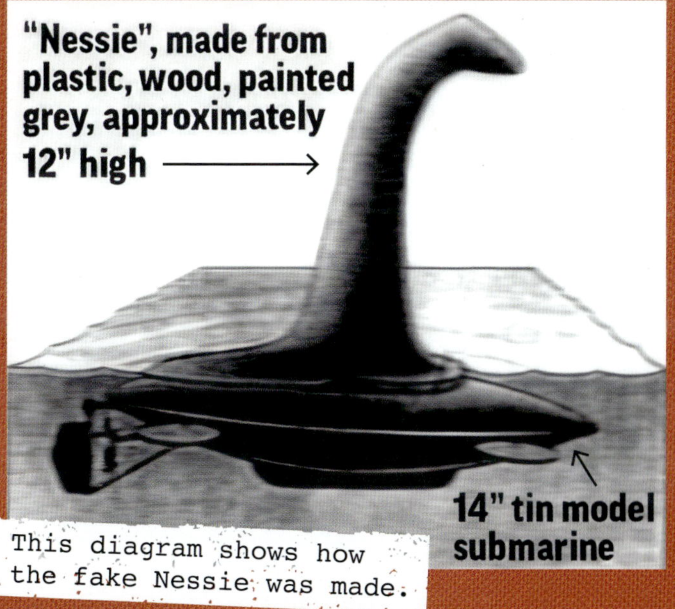


This diagram shows how the fake Nessie was made.

A lot of people continued to report seeing Nessie. Richard Horan worked in a boathouse on the lake. He reported seeing Nessie in June 1934. Three more people claimed they saw the monster that same day!

A tourist took this photo of Loch Ness in 1934. They claimed Nessie was the object swimming in the water.

This photo was also taken in 1934. But there is no source. Do you think it's real?

CHAPTER 2

# SEARCHING FOR EVIDENCE

Fast-forward to 1972. A group of researchers decided to learn more. Robert Rines led a team of scientists from America to Scotland. They used underwater photography and **sonar** to search the lake.

The sonar picked up a large moving object. The camera captured two photos of a large flipper. Some scientists believed the flipper could be from a plesiosaur! But no one knows for sure.

Sonar uses sound waves to find objects underwater. This image of a flipper puzzled the scientists.

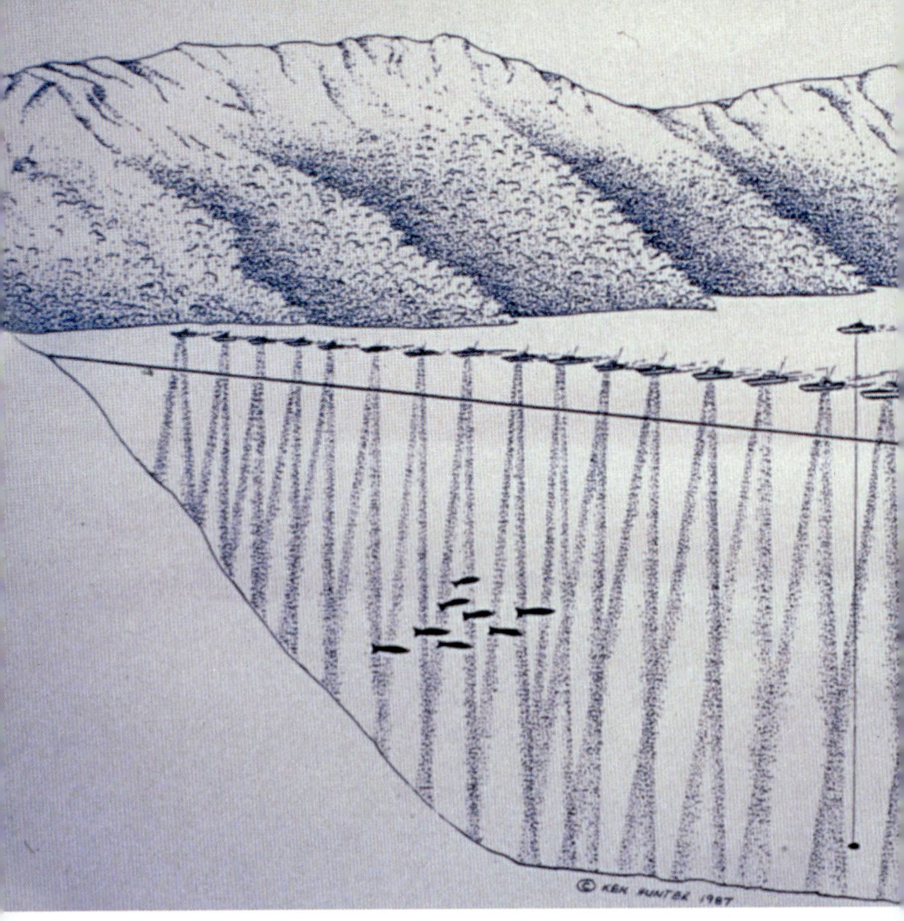


Another group of scientists searched the lake in 1987. It was called Operation Deepscan. Lead scientist Adrian Shine gathered twenty-four boats. They used sonar to scan Loch Ness for two days. Three times, the sonar picked up large, unknown objects. Could they have been Nessie?

This is an illustration of Operation Deepscan from 1987. The underwater lines represent the boats' sonar.

Shine went back ten years later with another team. Again sonar picked up an unknown object. Scientists on the boat believed it was an animal about 15 feet (4.6 m) long. But nobody could confirm what type of animal it was.

Do you think this European conger eel could be mistaken for Nessie?

There are other possible explanations for Nessie. Scientists have found **DNA** from different eels in the water of Loch Ness. The monster could be a European conger eel. This type of eel can grow to 10 feet (3 m) long. It can weigh 350 pounds (159 kg). That is about the same size as an American alligator.

# BURACH-BHAOI

An eel is also the subject of an old Scottish story. It is said to live in the water around the mountains near Loch Ness. It is known as the Burach-Bhaoi. This mysterious eel-like creature has nine eyes. It hides near paths and roadways. It will attack passersby. And it has a taste for blood. Could this be the same monster from Loch Ness?

It is said the Burach-Bhaoi drowns its victims.

Animals aren't the only theory to explain the sightings. Some people think Nessie could be explained by **seiches**. These are a type of wave caused by wind. They are common in Loch Ness.

The wind pushes warm water down into the cold water below. The water then bounces back. This wave motion could look like a creature from far away. What do you think?

Waves like these could also be caused by passing boats.

CHAPTER 3

# MODERN REPORTS

Nessie sightings continued as scientists searched for answers. Val Moffat reported seeing the creature in 1990. She was driving by Loch Ness on a bright, sunny day. She saw a large brownish-green lump in the water. She said it was about 30 feet (9 m) long.

Val Moffat noticed this lump in the water. She said it looked like an overturned boat.

Charlotte Robinson was twelve years old when she visited Loch Ness in 2018. She took a photo of a creature. "It had a neck and [its] head was in the shape of a hook," Charlotte said. Charlotte and her family were convinced that something big was living in the lake!

Charlotte took this photo with her cell phone.

**Drones** have also captured video above Loch Ness. Richard Mavor was filming kayakers on the lake in August 2021. That's when he noticed a weird figure in the water. His drone captured footage of a creature. It was about 30 feet (9 m) long. He claimed it was Nessie.

Look closely! You can just make out the shadow of something in the water. It is longer than a kayak.

## HOAX ALERT!

Researchers studied the footage. The figure wasn't moving. They said the creature was fake. Mavor had added an image to the video. It was of a plesiosaur he had found online.

Mavor used an image of a plesiosaur like this one.

The side-by-side gray shadows are the waves. What else could have made them?

There is even more recent evidence. A webcam captured two waves in September 2024. Some people believe they were made by two large creatures. Could there be more than one monster?

A month later, a sea captain was out on his boat. His name was Shaun Sloggie. A large, mysterious shape appeared on his sonar. "We've seen all sorts of fish . . . but this? This was different," Sloggie said. He believes it was the Loch Ness monster.

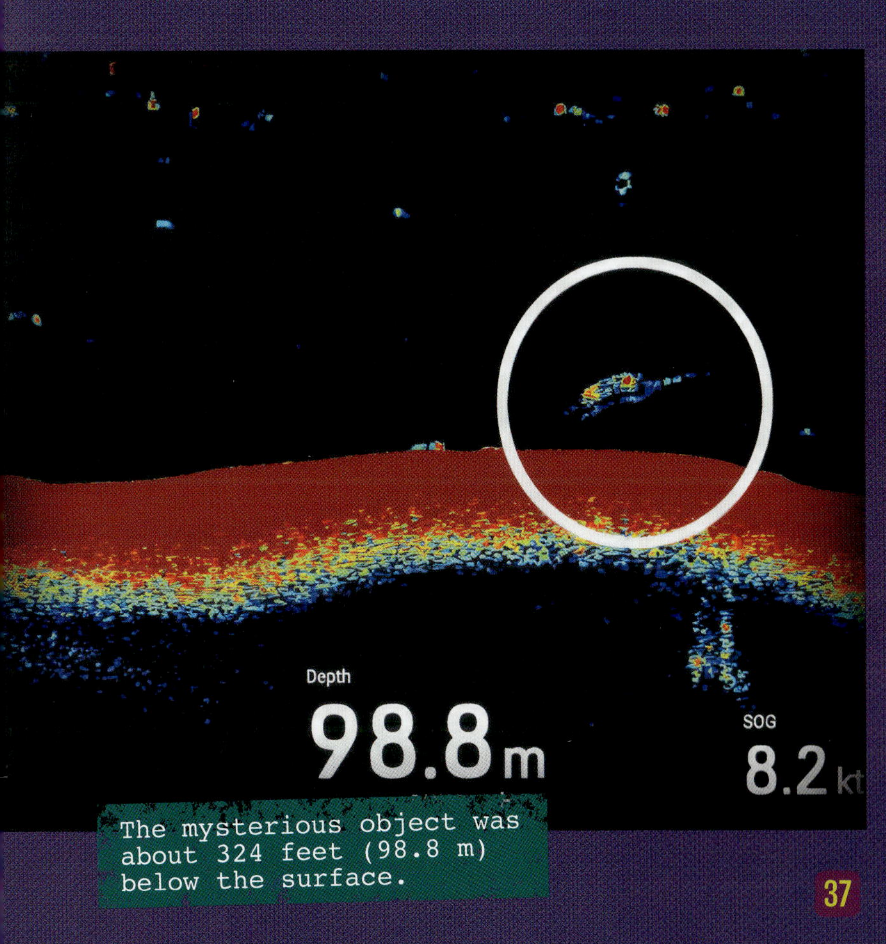


The mysterious object was about 324 feet (98.8 m) below the surface.

Technology is helping to search the dark waters of the lake. Equipment is being used to detect underwater sounds. Drones and webcams are watching the water. They are capturing more images.

Fort Augustus is a small Scottish village. It is at the southern end of Loch Ness.

The Loch Ness Centre in Scotland has asked NASA for help. They have strong cameras that can help scan the lake. NASA has not yet agreed to join the search. But the hunt continues . . .

# WHAT TO BELIEVE?

People have been looking for the Loch Ness monster for almost one hundred years. There are about twenty sightings a year. More than one in four people in Scotland believe the monster is real!

The country also makes a lot of money from tourists. Nessie brings in nearly $80 million a year. Local businesses benefit from keeping the story alive.

These are even more photos that claim to be of the Loch Ness monster.

So, is the Loch Ness monster real? We don't know. But it's important to question what we do know. Why? Because some people lie. They want to become famous with fake photos and videos.

The water in Loch Ness is cold year round. It stays at about 40°F (4°C).

Or they want to make money. The mystery will remain unsolved until there is more proof. What do you think? Maybe you're not sure. Maybe we can all agree that Nessie makes for a great story, real or not!

# TIMELINE: Then and Now

A story is written about Saint Columba and a water beast.

George Spicer reports a sighting to a local newspaper.

A newspaper publishes the "Surgeon's Photo."

565 BC | MAY 1933 | JULY 1933 | DECEMBER 1933 | APRIL 1934

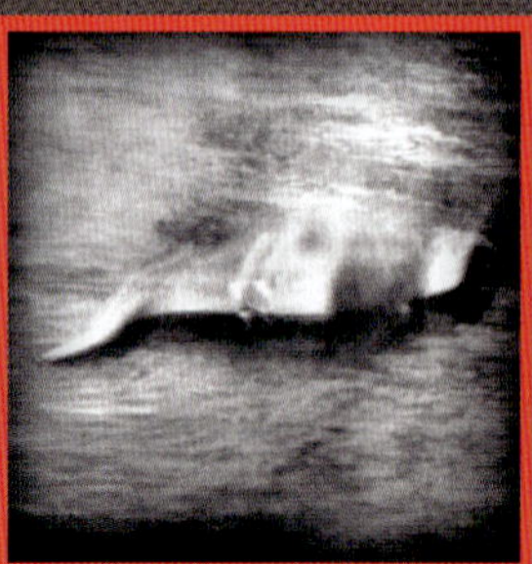

Newspaper reports Aldie Mackay's sighting in Loch Ness.

Duke Wetherell creates fake Nessie tracks.

**JUNE 1934**

Richard Horan and three others spot the monster the same day.

**AUGUST 1972**

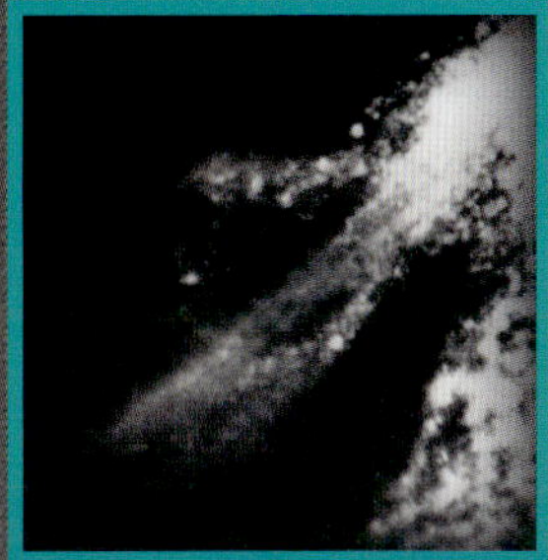

Researchers take photos of a creature's flipper.

**OCTOBER 1987**

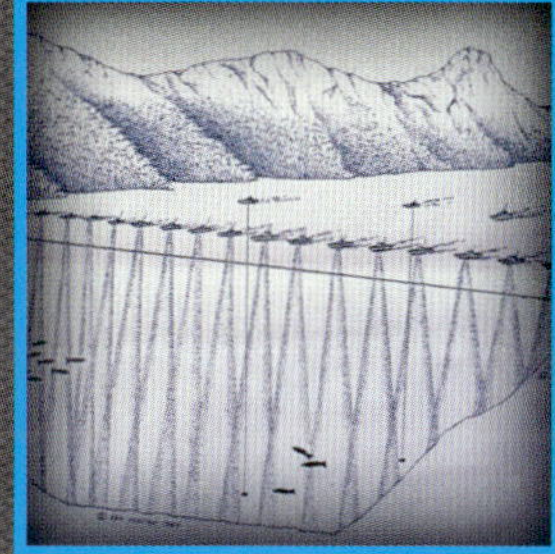

Operation Deepscan searches the lake.

**AUGUST 2018**

Charlotte Robinson takes a photo of Nessie.

**OCTOBER 2024**

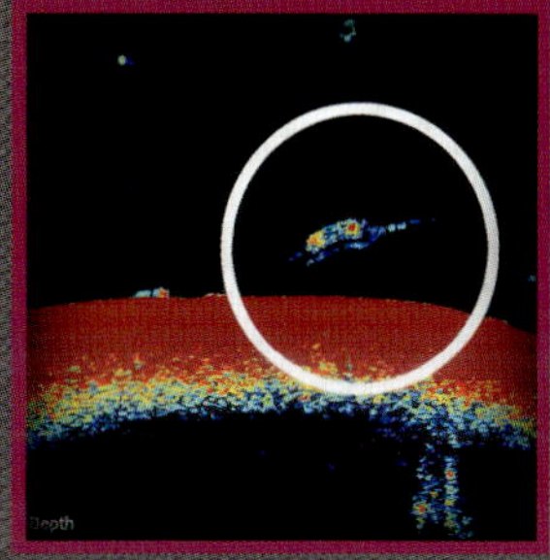

The sonar on Shaun Sloggie's boat picks up a large creature.

# EXTINCT CREATURES?

Some people believe that Nessie is a plesiosaur. It could be true. Here are two creatures that scientists thought were extinct. But they were later found to be still alive!

Coelacanth

The coelacanth was a bony fish that lived millions of years ago. One was found off the coast of South Africa in 1938.

The Chacoan peccary looks like a pig. But it is an ancient creature. Some were found living in the 1970s in Paraguay, Bolivia, and Argentina.

Chacoan peccary

# GLOSSARY

**cast** (kast) to form something by pouring soft or liquid material into a mold

**CE** "Common Era," used to refer to the years after the birth of Jesus Christ

**DNA** the molecule that carries our genes, found inside the nucleus of cells

**drone** (drohn) an aircraft without a pilot that is controlled remotely

**extinct** (ik-STINGKT) no longer found alive; known about only through fossils or history

**hoax** (hohks) a trick that makes people believe something that is not true

**monk** (muhngk) a man who lives apart from society in a religious community according to strict rules

**prehistoric** (pree-hi-STOR-ik) belonging to a time before history was recorded in written form

**seiche** (saysh) a wave on the surface of a lake or landlocked bay

**sonar** (SOH-nahr) an instrument used on ships and submarines that sends out underwater sound waves to determine the location of objects and the distance to the bottom

# INDEX



## ABOUT THE AUTHOR


Dinah Williams, who loves all things spooky and mysterious, has written more than a dozen books for kids, including *Amazing Immortals*; *Terrible but True*: *Awful Events in American History*; *True Hauntings: Deadly Disasters*; *Spooky Cemeteries*, which won a 2009 Children's Choice Book of the Year Award; and the Unsolved series: *Amelia Earhart*, *Bigfoot*, *Captain Kidd's Treasure*, and *Pyramids of Egypt*.